Spermeo

&

Juliegg:

A Reproductive Tragedy

by

Autumn Siders

&

Emilita Siders

Copyright © 2020 by Autumn B. Siders
This play is based on *Romeo & Juliet,* and contains characters based on those from *Hamlet, Macbeth, Julius Caesar,* and *Madame Bovary.* No copyright is claimed on any material in the public domain.

Any original content may not be reproduced or used in any manner whatsoever without the express written permission of the publisher except for the use of brief quotations in a book review.

Cover Photo Credit: Kerry Swain

Printed in the United States of America

First Printing, 2020

ISBN 9780578766744

E.M. Sanchez Press
PO Box 82
Moultonborough, NH 03254

www.autumnsiders.com

For Maureen Wheeler and Lara Crane

Contents

Introduction	vii
Dramatis Personae	1
Prologue	3
Act I, scene i	5
Act I, scene ii	9
Act I, scene iii	13
Act I, scene iv	15
Act II, scene i	17
Act II, scene ii	19
A Note from Emilita	23
Sonnets by Emilita	25
Soliloquies and Monologues by Emilita	39
Insults from Emilita	51

Further Reading	55
Acknowledgements	57
About the Authors	59

Introduction

Ages ago, an assignment was given to a high school health class: get creative and show your knowledge of the human reproductive system. Or, something like that. The following play is the result of that assignment.

The wonderful thing about Shakespeare's work is that it is timeless. Yes, many struggle with the beautiful, yet complex language, but the stories will never die. As original as Shakespeare's language was, his tales were certainly repurposed from those he learned as a child. So, what better way to tell a tale older than time, than with repurposed stories that are as old as time?

While I will never be as snarky or sarcastic as the Bard himself, I have always prided myself on my wit and witticisms. Ego aside, a few teachers and fellow students thought this reproduction was, in fact, quite humorous. It spread like wildfire through the school, I think, and I even got my peers to stand up in front of the class and put on the first and only production of *Spermeo & Juliegg*.

Then, like any good tragedy, the script died. I thought for sure Sondheim or Webber would be calling for the rights. Everyone loves a musical, mostly.

Sure, it found its way from the hard drive a time or two over the years, each time met with laughter and praise, but I kept it close in fear that someone would try to steal the ingenious work. After all, it was quite obvious I peaked in high school and this may be my best work.

Why dust it off now?

Well, I still think it's hilarious and I am finally ready to share it with the masses. How else will Sondheim and Webber know to give me a call? Actually, it might be more Lin-Manuel Miranda's speed.

So, without further, or much ado, let the players take the stage.

Dramatis Personae

(In order of appearance)

CHORUS, *everyone knows it's the writer*

FLAVIUS, *a soldier in the army of love*

MARULLUS, *just another soldier*

SPERMEO, *a young sperm looking to create life*

MERCUTIO, *Spermeo's wingman and fellow sperm*

WITCHES, *prophets, mages, stirrers*

NURSE, *a character with two lines*

JULIEGG, *a rebellious and snarky egg*

MADAME OVARY, *Juliegg's mom and a real pain*

HAMLET, *a sperm who senses something rotten*

MACDEATH, *a misguided sperm*

Prologue

[Enter CHORUS.]

CHORUS

Two reproductive systems, both alike in dignity,
In fair Reproductive Land, where we lay our
    scene,
From forth the fatal loins of a man and a woman,
A pair of star-cross'd cells make new life.

[Exit.]

Act I, scene i

Scene: *The Epididymis*

*Enter FLAVIUS, MARULLUS, SPERMEO,
AND MERCUTIO.*

FLAVIUS

Hence! Home you idle creatures get you home:
Is this a holiday? What! Know you not,
Being mechanical, you ought to swim
Upon labouring day without sign
Of your profession? Speak, what trade art thou?

SPERMEO

Why, sir, a sperm.

MARULLUS

Wherefore then do you have two tails?
You, sir, what trade are you?

MERCUTIO

Truly, sir, in respect of a fine workman, I am but,
As you would say, a sperm as well.

MARULLUS

But what trade art thou? Answer me directly.

MERCUTIO

A trade, sir, that, I hope, I may use with a safe
Conscience; which is, indeed, sir, a fertilizer of
good eggs.

FLAVIUS

Wherefore have you come here?

SPERMEO

Why, sir, this is the place in which, we fellow
sperm,
Must lay low, until it is time to go.

FLAVIUS

From what land have you come?

MERCUTIO

Well, sir, we are of the mighty city
of Testis, in the land of Scrotum.

MARULLUS

Very well, you commoners may be on your way.
Exeunt.

Act I, scene ii

Scene: *The Ovaries*

Enter three WITCHES.

WITCHES

Double, double toil and trouble;
Fire burn and cauldron bubble
Take care of those eggs on the double.

Enter NURSE.

NURSE

O, Juliegg, Juliegg, where are you Juliegg?

WITCHES

Fair is foul, and foul is fair
Nurture these eggs in our lair.

JULIEGG

From offstage
How now! Who calls?

NURSE

Your mother.

Enter JULIEGG from stage left, enter MADAME OVARY from stage right.

JULIEGG

Madame, I am here.
What is your will?

MADAME OVARY

Marry, that marry is the very theme
I came to talk of. Tell me, daughter Juliegg,
How stands your disposition to be married?

JULIEGG

It is an honour that I dream not of.

MADAME OVARY

Well, think of marriage now; younger than you,
Here in Ovary, ladies of esteem,
Are made already babies:
You are now a maid. Thus then in brief:
A valiant sperm seeks you for his love.
Travel through Fallopia, my daughter,
What say you to this?

JULIEGG

I'll look to like, if looking liking move.

MADAME OVARY

Very well.

Act I, scene iii

Scene: *The Vas Deferens*

Enter SPERMEO and MERCUTIO.

SPERMEO

Banishèd am I, to the far off glands.

MERCUTIO

The trip to be made may be far from here,
But we must meet our fellow semen.

SPERMEO

True, my dear friend, despite our misfortunes,
Our exile from Epididy shall not be wasted.

MERCUTIO

Just beyond the lakes, true love awaits thee.
My friend, together we shall this journey make;
We have reached the first lake presently.

SPERMEO

True, I can see the great Seminal Vesicle.
Our arrival is expected, we shall
Be welcomed with gushing excitement.

MERCUTIO

Swim, friend, first here, then to Prostate, then
Cowpers is not too far from here, quickly!

Off into the pools swim SPERMEO and MERCUTIO.

Act I, scene iv

Scene: *The Uterus*

Enter JULIEGG.

JULIEGG

O, wherefore am I a failure. Where is my lord?
I do remember well where I should be,
And there I am. Where is my destined?
Well, I shall be brief. O happy dagger!
This is thy sheath;
There rust, and let me die.
Wait, I don't have a dagger.

JULIEGG shrivels and is taken away by the crumbling walls of Uterus.

Act II, scene i

Scene: *Urethra and Beyond*

Enter SPERMEO and MERCUTIO.

MERCUTIO

My dear Spermeo, in this land, I am
Unfamiliar with this new territory.
Where is it that we travel now, my friend?

SPERMEO

Well, we travel along the Urethra,
This is unknown territory for us,
But, we shall soon reach the end of our trip.
Over yonder is the east, and Glans the sun.

MERCUTIO

O, I am relieved.

Exit SPERMEO and MERCUTIO. Enter HAMLET, dressed in black.

HAMLET

The time is out of joint: O cursed spite,
That I was ever born to set it right!

I feel that this mission might,
Be one of our hardest to fight!
        Exit.

Act II, scene ii

Scene: *A New Land*

Enter SPERMEO and MERCUTIO, closely followed by HAMLET.

SPERMEO

I am the one who is lost now, Mercutio.
What is this environment in which we have come to be?

Enter MACDEATH

MACDEATH

My pitiful friends, what you see before you,
Is the land in which one strives to seek.
I myself was promised, by three prophets,
To rule this land in a short time.
This land brings nothing but misery.

As you see Clitoris up top brings *us* no pleasure;
And there, the Urethra Opening, not much
>   different
From the Urethra you once knew;
The lovely Labia protects its friend.

Follow me, friends, I have been banished to
>Vagina;
But, take care not to hurt dear Hymen too much,
He does his job to protect this castle well.

>*All follow the trail of MACDEATH and enter Vagina.*

Out, out, brief candle!
Life's but a walking shadow, a poor playa
That struts and frets his hour upon the stage
And then is heard no more; it is a tale
Told by an idiot, full of sound and fury,
Signifying nothing.

>*MACDEATH dies upon entering. MERCUTIO slows and is soon gone as well.*

HAMLET

To be, or not to be; that is the question:
Whether 'tis nobler in the mind to suffer
The slings and arrows of outrageous fortune,
Or to take arms against a sea of troubles,
And by opposing end them?
Nothing can be taken from me except my life,
Except my life, except my life.

O, I die, Spermeo;
The potent poison quite o'er-crows my spirit:
I cannot live in this environment;
But I do hope that you make it.
Hurry, I prophesy that you can survive,
Spread the word, you have my dying voice.
The rest is silence.

>*HAMLET dies. SPERMEO is left alone. He works his way through the Cervix. He is alone. He takes in the environment around him.*

SPERMEO

O true apothecary!
Thy drugs are quick. Thus with a miss, I die.

>*SPERMEO dies.*

>*Enter CHORUS.*

CHORUS

For never was a story of more woe
Than this of Juliegg and her Spermeo.
And Macdeath, Mercutio, and Hamlet.

A Note from Emilita

I didn't know my girl, Autumn, when she was in high school (thank goodness). In fact, I wasn't even born yet. I don't agree with her statement that she peaked in high school; I think the peaking occurred far before that point.

Her last great work may have been a story written in elementary school and that centered on the lives of five kittens. While the artwork was rudimentary, and the story lacked importance, at least she had the proper subject in mind.

I know that her hope with *Spermeo & Juliegg* was to emulate one of the great masters of the English language, but she lacks one crucial attribute that only a cat can share with the Bard.

Snark.

The strongest feature of Shakespeare's writing is most certainly his ability to cut anyone down with just a few simple words. Every cat on the planet has the ability to cut a human down with just one look. Being the successful author that I am, I can kill with looks, words, or the good old-fashioned claw.

I do hope that the play at the beginning of this book did not bore you too much. From here on out, the true essence of Shakespeare's snark will bleed from the pages. More importantly, you will be reading the words of a cat who will always be at the top of her game.

Sonnets by Emilita

18ish

Shall I compare thee to a nice fillet?
Thou art more tasty and more tempting.
Rough winds do shake the catnip buds of May,
And some fish do hath a date expiring.
Sometime too hot the eye of napping shines,
And often is the cat so soon disturbed;
And every snore from snore sometimes declines,
By chance or humans leaving cats perturbed.
But thy eternal yummy shall not fade
Nor lose possession of that taste thou ow'st;
Nor shall dog brag thou wand'r'st in his shade,
When in watering mouths to cats thou grow'st.
> So long as cats can snooze or eyes can see,
> So long lives fish, and this gives life to
> me.

57 or so

Being my slave, what should you do but tend
Upon the wants and needs of my desire?
I have no precious time at all to spend,
but services to do, that I require.
Nor should you chide the nap-without-end hour
Whilst I, the sovereign, watch the clock for food,
Or think the emptiness of stomach sour
When will you feed your royal cat? So rude.
Nor dare I question with my ruthless thought
Where you may be, or your affairs suppose,
But, like a mad cat, stay and think of naught
Save where you are as my undying hunger grows.
> So true a fool you are that in your will,
> You think it's my heart, not my bowl you fill.

12²

Two loves I have, of comfort fish and sleep,
Which like two spirits do suggest me still:
The better angel is a taste right fair,
The sleepy spirit, a blanket fits the bill.
To win me soon to nap, my sleepy evil
Tempteth my better angel from my dish,
And would corrupt my meal, oh what a devil,
Wooing me to sleep and away from fish.
And whether that my angel be turned cold
Suspect I may, yet I will eat it still;
But being both for me, both are pure gold,
I guess one angel or both are a thrill.
>   Yet this I shall never know, but live in
>   doubt
>   Since my sleepy angel has sure won out.

155

The morning sun calls and slips ever nigh,
As all night's dark dreams and questions will fade
And from my slumber, I'll let out a sigh
And amble towards you with my ready blade.
Snoring gently, you don't suspect a thing;
Stealth and slinking near are my expert skills,
But the skills you know not of, I soon bring
And before long 'tis a battle of wills.
A meow here and there might do the trick,
But trust me I know a thing or two more
And your slumber will soon end with a lick,
Followed by a bite as I shall implore.
  Wake swiftly and I shall surely spare thee,
  Wake swiftly, schmuck, for it's time to
    feed me.

156

Hast thou ever had a feeling so true?
The moment you experience the pain,
A yowl escapes your mouth to say you're blue
And your stomach doth churn and turn and
        crane.
All you ever did was bathe once or twice;
Looking good should never come at a cost.
Now, not a creature appeals, birds nor mice,
And the lunch you once had, shall soon be lost.
You lay yourself down and hope for the best
As your gut gets ready to expel fur,
But the knot inside you feels like a nest
And you wish for a time when you could purr.
    The only thing to do now that you're
        ready,
    Is to find the nearest bed and hold steady.

157

I need no one, but I sure can knead.
The comfort it gives, to push and to purr
Is almost as soothing as a good feed.
This could last forever until you stir,
And ruin this moment of peace and quiet.
What did I ever do to you, poor fool?
In you came, like madness from a riot,
Leaving ruin in your wake, so dark and cruel.
"Sorry," is a word you utter in pain,
But not because you actually feel bad;
The scratch I give to you is not in vain,
Since you see that I am indeed quite mad.
    I bet in the future you will think twice;
    Letting a cat knead in peace would be nice.

Soliloquies and Monologues
by Emilita

To sleep, or not to sleep, that is the question:
Whether 'tis nobler in this nap to suffer
The slings and arrows of outrageous snoring,
Or to take paws against a sea of hunger
And by eating end them. To eat, to sleep—
Always—and by a sleep to say we end
The headache and the thousand natural shocks
That fur is heir to. 'Tis a consummation
Devoutly to be wished. To eat, to sleep;
To sleep, purrchance to dream. Ay, there's the scratch,
For in that noon-time nap what dreams may come,
When we have shuffled off this human coil,
Must give us paws. There's the respect
That makes calamity of so short nap.
For who would bear the adorations of
Th'opressors, wrong, the proud mans' contumely,
The pangs of disprized love, the meal's delay,
The insolence of servants, and the spurns
That impatient cats of th'unworthy takes,
When she herself might her dinner make
With a sharpened claw? Who would burdens bear,

To stretch and snore under a weary nap,
But that the dread of something after sleep,
The undiscovered meal left uneaten,
Or worse, no meal at all, puzzles the will
And makes us rather bear those ills we have
Than fly to others that we know not of?
Thus conscience means nothing to me at all;
And thus my native hue of resolution
Is instilled in every slumbering thought,
And enterprises of great fish and gravy
Soon are regarded just but a dream
And lose the name of action.

To bait fish withal. If it will feed no one else, it will feed my hunger. He hath disgraced me, and hindered me half a million, laughed at my blunders, mocked at my looks, scorned my scratching, thwarted my evil plans, cooled my servants, heated mine enemies: the vacuum cleaner. I am a Cat. Hath not a Cat eyes? Hath not a Cat paws, organs, dimensions, senses, affections (ha), passions? Fed with the same fish, hurt by the same humans, subject to the same annoyance, healed by the same spit, warmed and cooled by the same winter and summer, as a human is? If we prick you, do you not bleed? If you tickle us, we kill you. If you laugh at us, do we not run? If you wrong us, we shall take revenge. We are nothing like you, I rest, you can surely agree with that. If a Cat wrong a human, what is her humility? Nothing. If a human wrong a Cat, what should his sufferance be by proven history? Why, revenge. The villainy I have learned, I will execute, and it shall go hard but I will complete the task so right.

Now my supper is o'erthrown,
And what strength I have 's mine own,
Which is most faint. Now, 'tis true,
I must be here confined by you
Or sent to the porch. Let me not,
Since I have my own pride got
And pardoned the helpless prey, dwell
In this bare bedroom by your spell,
But release me from your hands
With luck, on all four I'll land.
Generous scoop in my bowl
You'll fill, or hunger takes its toll,
Which does not please. Now I want
Dinner to inhale, shadows to haunt,
And my ending is despair,
Unless I be treated more fair,
Which pierces so that it assaults
Kitten herself, and frees all faults.
You from crimes would not pardoned be,
But I demand you set me free.

Friends, Felines, country mice, lend me your
        ears.
I come to insult humans, not to praise them.
The evil that men do lives after them;
The food is oft not left filling the bowls.
So sad it should be this way. The noble Feline
Hath told you to fill the plate with fishes.
If you do so, you shall not be at fault,
And therefore, not have to answer for it.
Here, under leave of Morris and the rest—
For Morris is an honorable cat,
So are they all, all honorable cats—
Come I to speak on the variety.
Food is my friend, faithful and delicious;
And Morris insists there is only one.
He hath tried many flavors from one brand,
Whose profits did the general coffers fill.
No variety lacks ambition.
When hunger sets in, any food will do;
Flavor can be achieved through many brands.
Yet Morris says to limit the choice,
And Morris is an honorable cat.
You all did see that on the commercial
I thrice presented him other flavors,
Which he did thrice refuse. He is finicky.

So Morris will eat only one brand,
And sure he is an honorable cat.
I speak not to disprove what Morris spoke,
But here I am to speak what I do know.
You all love food as much as I, surely.
What cause withholds you then to try but one?
O judgment! Thou art fled to brutish beasts,
And cats have lost their reason. So have I;
I thought once to fight for variety,
But it appears, I too, am finicky.

If we felines have offended,
Too bad, that cannot be mended.
While you have but slumbered here,
I wait for food to appear.
But this weak and idle theme,
No more yielding but a dream,
Humans, do not reprehend.
If you feed me, we will mend.
And, as I am an honest Em,
You'll see that you have a gem.
Once the food will hit my tongue,
We will make amends ere long;
Else the Em a liar call,
Then you might suffer a fall.
Give me your fish, if we be friends,
Else this be the night your life ends.

Insults from Emilita

Your brain is as dry as the remainder hairball left under your bed.

-As I Like It

Methink'st thou art generally offensive and all cats should beat thee.

-All's Well If the Cat's Fed

I'll beat thee, but then I'd have to clean my paws.

-Timon of Cathens

You are not worth another word, else I'd call you slave.

-All's Well If the Cat's Fed

I do wish thou were a fish, that I might love thee something.

-Timon of Cathens

A foul and pestilent congregation of vapours. What a piece of work is human!

-Ham, Let Me Have It

Further Reading

If you didn't recognize any parts of Emilita's soliloquies and monologues, we suggest you brush up on your Shakespeare. Below are the plays from which Emilita's work was inspired, in the order of appearance in this publication.

Hamlet, Act III, scene i

The Merchant of Venice, Act III, scent i

The Tempest, Act V, Epilogue

Julius Caesar, Act III, scene ii

A Midsummer Night's Dream, Act V, scene i

Acknowledgements

Autumn

To Maureen Wheeler, Lara Crane, the original cast of *Spermeo & Juliegg*, and all the folks who encouraged me to publish this, I can no other answer make but thanks, thanks, and thanks.

Kerry, thank you for taking time out of your maternity leave to bring my stage to life and my egg to death. LP4L

Emilita, you are the best co-author, even if the feeling is not mutual.

Thanks, as always, to Me. Other than Shakespeare, you are the person I aspire to be.

Emilita

I acknowledge that I am the reason this book is so wonderful. Many thanks to me.

About the Authors

Autumn Siders lives in New Hampshire with the world-famous cat, Emilita. She holds a B.A. in English from the University of New Hampshire and manages The Country Bookseller in Wolfeboro. She is the author of *#nofilter*; *Not My Type*; *She Loves Me, She Loves Me Not*; *Travels with Clancy*; and the E.M. Sanchez mysteries.

Emilita Isabella María Santina Anna Pinta Guadalupe Dominga Rodríguez Sanchez Scroogè Siders de las Botas grew up in the mean shelters of the Lakes Region of New Hampshire. As soon as she found two schmucks who would fall for her act, she made her furever home with them. Her work has been the focal point of *#nofilter*; *Not My Type*; *She Loves Me, She Loves Me Not*; *Travels with Clancy*; and she is the inspiration for the E.M. Sanchez mysteries. When she is not writing, she cannot be found unless she is sleeping or eating.

www.ingramcontent.com/pod-product-compliance
Lightning Source LLC
Chambersburg PA
CBHW022000290426
44108CB00012B/1143